D1192692

WITHDRAWN

EXPLORERS DISCOVERING THE WORLD

THE EXPLORATION OF

SOUTH AMERICA

Tim Cooke

Gareth Stevens
Publishing

Please visit our website, www.garethstevens.com. For a free color catalog of all our high-quality books, call toll-free 1-800-542-2595 or fax 1-877-542-2596.

Library of Congress Cataloging-in-Publication Data

Cooke, Tim.
 The exploration of South America / Tim Cooke.
     p. cm. — (Explorers discovering the world)
 Includes index.
ISBN 978-1-4339-8628-4 (pbk.)
ISBN 978-1-4339-8629-1 (6-pack)
ISBN 978-1-4339-8627-7 (library binding)
1. South America—Discovery and exploration—Juvenile literature. 2. Explorers—South America—History—Juvenile literature. I. Title.
 E121.C67 2013
 980'.01—dc23

                    2012034534

Published in 2013 by
Gareth Stevens Publishing
111 East 14th Street, Suite 349
New York, NY 10003

© 2013 Brown Bear Books Ltd

For Brown Bear Books Ltd:
Editorial Director: Lindsey Lowe
Managing Editor: Tim Cooke
Children's Publisher: Anne O'Daly
Art Director: Jeni Child
Designer: Lynne Lennon
Picture Manager: Sophie Mortimer

Picture Credits
Front Cover: Shutterstock: Jo Way main; **Thinkstock:** Photos.com inset.

Corbis: Bettmann 18; David Torres Costales/@DavoTC 42; **Library of Congress:** 13, 32; **Public Domain:** 7, 11, 19, 35, 41, 43; **Robert Hunt Library:** 10, Naval Museum of Madrid 6; **Shutterstock:** 8, 40, Antonio Abrignani 21, Andrej Glucks 30, Janne Hamalainen 38, Stanislav Spurny 26, Anibal Trejo 27, Jo Way 20; **Thinkstock:** Comstock 45, Hemera 5t, 15, istockphoto 5b, 9, 22, 24, 25, 28, 31, 33, 34, 36, 37, 39, 44, Photos.com 14, 16, 17, Zoonar 12; **Topfoto:** Rose Deakin 29, The Granger Collection 23.

Brown Bear Books has made every attempt to contact copyright holders. If anyone has any information please contact smortimer@windmillbooks.co.uk

All rights reserved. No part of this book may be reproduced, stored in a retrieval system, or transmitted in any form or by any means, electronic, mechanical, photocopying, recording, or otherwise, without the prior written permission of the copyright holder.

Manufactured in the United States of America
1 2 3 4 5 6 7 8 9 12 11 10

CPSIA compliance information: Batch #CW13GS: For further information contact Gareth Stevens, New York, New York at 1-800-542-2595.

CONTENTS

INTRODUCTION

From 1492, when Christopher Columbus first made landfall in the "New World," the Spanish were eager to explore and claim possession of the rich new territories. Drawn by stories of a fabled city of gold, bands of conquistadors sailed for the new lands. They wanted territory and treasure.

The Aztec Empire of Central America and the Inca Empire of Peru were indeed rich in treasure. Within a few years, the Spaniards had destroyed these mighty civilizations. They built their own colonies and sent cargoes of gold, silver, and gemstones back to Spain.

Later Explorers

Meanwhile, other explorers charted the new lands. Later, particularly in the Portuguese colony of Brazil, missionaries led exploration. They traveled deep into the interior of South America, seeking to convert native peoples to Christianity. They were followed by a generation of scientists eager to discover the secrets of the plant and animal life of the Amazon rain forest.

This Maya temple stands in Chichén Itzá in Mexico. The Spaniards destroyed most Aztec and Maya temples and forced the people to convert to Christianity.

A road zigzags up a steep slope to the Inca city of Machu Picchu. Such strongholds were so remote in the Andes that the Spaniards never found them.

1493–1494

DIVIDING THE NEW WORLD

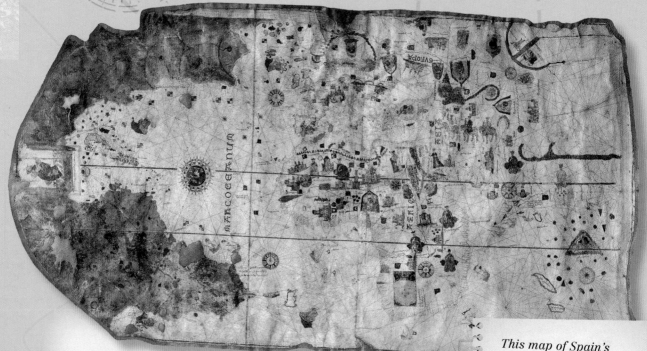

This map of Spain's territories in the New World was created in 1550. It was based on the voyages of the Spanish sailor Juan de la Cosa.

When Christopher Columbus "discovered" the Americas in 1492, he was sailing on behalf of Spain. Both Spain and its seafaring rival, Portugal, sent expeditions to map and explore the new lands. Both countries wanted the "New World" and its resources for themselves.

DID YOU KNOW?

Columbus was trying to find a fast route to China and Japan. Finding the Americas instead was a failure for him.

King Ferdinand and Queen Isabella of Spain asked the pope, Alexander VI, to allow Spanish expeditions to the New World to convert native peoples to Christianity. The Portuguese urged the pope to let them do the same thing.

Destiny Is Drawn

In May 1493, Alexander issued a decree. It split the new lands in the west between Spain and Portugal. Each country had the right to explore in its own part of South America. In 1494, the Treaty of Tordesillas confirmed the arrangement. The treaty had completely excluded the British and the Dutch, who were Europe's other great sea powers. They were furious at being left out.

TREATY OF TORDESILLAS

The 1494 treaty drew an imaginary line 900 miles (1,450 km) west of the Cape Verde Islands. Spain was entitled to lands to the west of the Cape Verde Islands. Portugal took any land to the east of the line. The treaty set the course of European exploration. Spain set up powerful colonies in the Caribbean, Mexico, and Peru. Portugal's lands in the New World were limited to what is now Brazil.

The Cabo (Cape) de la Vela in Colombia was discovered by Juan de la Cosa in 1499. He was on his fourth voyage to explore Spain's new lands.

AMERIGO VESPUCCI

Italian-born Amerigo Vespucci gave his name to America, even though he did not discover the continent. Vespucci claimed to have sailed on Columbus's second voyage, in 1493. He led his own expedition to the New World in 1497. He was the first European to see the mouth of the mighty Amazon River.

Amerigo Vespucci gave his name to a continent because a mapmaker wrongly believed the explorer had discovered it.

DID YOU KNOW?

America got its name in 1507 when Martin Waldseemüller used Vespucci's name on one of his maps.

Vespucci claimed to have landed on the Florida coast in 1497, although some historians believe his claim was false. Vespucci then sailed to Brazil as part of an expedition led by Alonso de Ojeda in 1499.

Influential Explorer

In 1501, King Manuel I of Portugal sent Vespucci back to South America. He sailed along the Brazilian coast, discovering Rio de Janeiro. When Vespucci got home, he wrote about his journeys. A German mapmaker named Martin Waldseemüller used his descriptions to produce up-to-date maps of the world. That made Vespucci more famous than other explorers who had actually discovered more important places.

Vespucci discovered and named Rio de Janeiro. The natural harbor would become the heart of the Portuguese Empire in South America.

CABRAL IN BRAZIL

Pedro Álvars Cabral was a Portuguese nobleman who is credited with discovering Brazil in 1500. He did it by accident. His fleet of 13 ships was intending to follow Vasco da Gama's route around Africa to India. Instead, Cabral sailed so far west out into the Atlantic that he made landfall on a previously unknown coast. He claimed the whole region for King Manuel I of Portugal.

1513–1519

VASCO NÚÑEZ DE BALBOA

Vasco Núñez de Balboa began his career as an explorer when he stowed away in a barrel on a ship. He was fleeing from debts he owed on the island of Hispaniola. Balboa was a natural leader. He soon found himself in charge of a group of settlers in Panama.

Balboa founded Darien in Panama and later crossed the narrow isthmus to reach the Pacific Ocean.

DID YOU KNOW?

Balboa was the first European to set eyes on the Pacific Ocean, when he crossed Panama in 1513.

This early map shows the isthmus of Panama, the narrowest point between the Atlantic and the Pacific Oceans. At its narrowest, the neck of land is only 30 miles (50 km) wide.

In Panama, Balboa founded Santa Maria de la Antigua del Darien, or Darien, the first major Spanish settlement on the mainland. The Spanish authorities said Balboa had illegally made himself governor. They threatened to punish him.

Searching for Gold

Balboa sailed the coast of Colombia and Panama searching for gold and slaves. In 1513, he heard about an ocean to the west. It was said to have more gold than Spain had iron. Eager to find it, Balboa gathered an expedition of 190 Spaniards plus about 1,000 slaves and guides. He hoped a great discovery might help him avoid punishment for taking control of Darien.

JEWISH SETTLERS

Some of the earliest settlers in Latin America were Jews fleeing religious persecution. The Spanish monarchs, King Ferdinand and Queen Isabella, only wanted Catholics to live in Spain. They persecuted Jews. In the new colonies, the Jews could openly practice their religion. Some were good businesspeople who developed strong trade links between the New and Old Worlds.

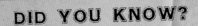

DID YOU KNOW?

Exploring the Pacific coastline, Balboa found pearl fisheries and gold. He sent the best pearls to the king in Spain.

Balboa found rich pearl fisheries on the Pacific coast. He planned to build new ships to harvest the valuable pearls and to search for gold.

The route he took was only 60 miles (100 km) to the "new" ocean, but it was hard. It lay through thick jungle and over steep hills and dangerous swamps. Balboa had to use force to defeat hostile peoples.

A New Ocean

Around September 25, Balboa climbed a peak. From the summit he could see the "South Sea," now called the Pacific Ocean. A few days later, he and his men reached the shore of the Gulf of San Miguel. He claimed the ocean for Spain.

Balboa found rich supplies of gold, pearls, and slaves on the coast. He took them back to Darien—but he was no longer in charge.

An Unhappy End

The authorities did not trust Balboa. The king appointed Pedro Arias Dávila as governor in his place. Dávila put Balboa on trial for seizing the governorship. In 1519, Balboa was found guilty and beheaded.

PEDRO ARIAS DÁVILA

Pedro Arias Dávila was originally friendly toward Balboa, but later had him executed. As governor, Dávila ruled Panama with great cruelty. He abandoned the settlement at Darien and founded a new capital at Panama City in 1519. From there, he sent out expeditions to explore north and south along the narrow stretch of land that separated the Caribbean Sea, which is part of the Atlantic, from the Pacific Ocean.

Balboa claims the Pacific Ocean and its provinces for Spain, on September 29, 1513. His journey across Panama took him about 70 miles (110 km) from Darien.

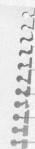

HERNÁN CORTÉS

Hernán Cortés was the Spaniard who defeated the mighty Aztec Empire of Mexico in 1521 with just 500 men and 16 horses. Fiercely loyal to the Spanish crown, Cortés belonged to a new type of explorer. They were the conquistadors, or conquerors. They explored in search of gold and glory.

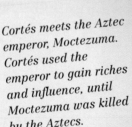

Cortés meets the Aztec emperor, Moctezuma. Cortés used the emperor to gain riches and influence, until Moctezuma was killed by the Aztecs.

DID YOU KNOW?

The Aztecs sacrificed thousands of humans to keep their sun god happy and to make sure he looked after them.

Some ruins of the Aztec capital, Tenochtitlán, can still be seen in the heart of downtown Mexico City. But most of the Aztec buildings were destroyed.

Cortés left Spain as a young man. He moved to Hispaniola and then Cuba to try to make his fortune. In 1519, he was put in charge of the first expedition to the mainland. He ignored an order from the governor of Cuba cancelling his appointment.

Allies Against the Aztec

Cortés landed in Yucatan, Mexico. The local Mayan people attacked, but the Spaniards defeated them. Many Maya died. Cortés then persuaded the Mayan chiefs to support him. He also made alliances with other local peoples against the Aztecs. The Maya gave Cortés a valuable asset: La Malinche, a slave girl who acted as his interpreter.

THE AZTEC EMPIRE

Between 1300 and 1519, when the Spanish arrived, the warlike Aztecs built a huge empire by conquering their neighbors. Aztec civilization was very sophisticated. The Spaniards were astonished by the paved roads and stone buildings of the capital, Tenochtitlán. But they were horrified to learn the Aztecs sacrificed thousands of people in ceremonies designed to keep their gods happy.

THE EXPLORATION OF SOUTH AMERICA

The Aztec emperor, Moctezuma, panicked at the news that Cortés had arrived. He sent gifts to the Spaniards to try to stop Cortés from attacking.

Marching to the Capital

After four months of preparation, Cortés marched on the Aztec capital, Tenochtitlán. To show his men he was serious, he destroyed his ships. In the capital, Moctezuma greeted them in a friendly way. He gave the Spaniards lavish gifts. But Cortés killed many Aztec nobles and took Moctezuma hostage.

DID YOU KNOW?

The Aztecs believed their god, the white-bearded Quetzalcoatl, would return. They thought Cortés might be the god.

Cortés's troops attack native warriors in this old illustration. Cortés fought with some peoples but made alliances with others against the Aztecs.

16

Spaniards build a cathedral on the site of Tenochtitlán. They pulled down Aztec temples and pyramids. They reused the stone to build a new capital, Mexico City.

The Empire Falls

Cortés headed to the coast to defeat a force sent from Cuba to stop him. The Aztecs rebelled against the men he left in Tenochtitlán. Cortés returned, but Moctezuma was killed by his own people. On July 1, 1520, the Spaniards fled the city. Many were killed. Cortés returned in May 1521 and laid siege to the city. After 93 days, the starving inhabitants surrendered. The Aztec Empire had fallen.

LA MALINCHE

Malinche means "stain" in Spanish. It is what some people call the native woman who acted as Cortés's interpreter. The Spaniards called her Dona Marina. Dona Marina was very smart. She spoke local languages, including the Aztec language, Nahuatl. She could tell Cortés what the Aztecs were planning. In 1525, she gave birth to his son.

1522–1533

FRANCISCO PIZARRO

The success of Hernán Cortés in Mexico fired up other Spanish conquistadors to search for gold in the New World. Francisco Pizarro was an illiterate peasant from the barren Spanish region of Extremadura. He would eventually bring down the vast Inca Empire of the Andes Mountains in Peru.

Francisco Pizarro first heard stories about the riches of "Biru"— Peru—while exploring Panama with Vasco Núñez de Balboa.

DID YOU KNOW?

Only 13 men from Pizarro's first voyage chose to join his second—successful— trip. The others returned to Panama.

Pizarro had arrived in the Americas as early as 1502, to search for gold and glory. Now, he and another explorer, Diego de Almagro, heard stories of fabulous riches in distant lands. In 1522, they set sail from Panama to the mainland. But on their first expedition they found nothing.

Dreams Come True

In 1526, Pizarro and Almagro tried again. They sailed along the coasts of Ecuador and Peru. They dropped anchor in a town called Tumbes, which was part of the Inca Empire. The Spaniards' wildest dreams came true. They found gold and silver, stone buildings and fine textiles.

THE INCA EMPIRE

In just a century, the Inca from the city of Cuzco built an empire of 12 million people in the Andes. The empire stretched 2,500 miles (4,000 km) through Peru and Ecuador into southern Colombia and northern Chile. The Inca built magnificent stone buildings without any cement. They built terraces to grow corn on mountainsides. Craftsmen made beautiful objects out of gold and silver.

Inca artists made remarkable gold and silver objects. In Cuzco, the Spaniards found a "garden" planted with gold and silver cobs of corn.

Pizarro was eager to explore the Inca Empire. He got royal approval from Spain to continue his exploration. He returned to Peru at the end of 1530 with a small party: just 180 men and 27 horses.

A Nation Divided

Pizarro found the Inca Empire in the middle of a civil war. Two brothers both claimed the throne. Late in 1532, Pizarro arranged to meet the victor, Atahualpa. The emperor was camped at Cajamarca with 30,000 warriors.

Remote Inca cities, like Machu Picchu, continued to exist after the fall of the empire in 1533. The last Inca emperor was executed by the Spanish in 1572.

This 19th-century image shows the funeral of Atahualpa. He was tried on false charges of treason and executed.

DID YOU KNOW?

The Inca had never seen horses before and were terrified of them; they also had no guns or gunpowder.

Fall of the Empire

In an ambush, Spaniards armed with muskets and crossbows massacred up to 10,000 Inca. Atahualpa was captured. In return for his freedom, he offered to fill his prison room with gold. The Spaniards took the gold but killed Atahualpa anyway. With the emperor dead, the Inca Empire fell apart. A year later, Pizarro arrived at the Inca capital, Cuzco. The empire had fallen as easily as the Aztec Empire to the north.

SECRET CITY

The Inca built the city of Machu Picchu high in a remote valley in the Andes, almost 8,000 feet (2,430 m) above sea level. The Spanish conquistadors never found it. That's why it is so well preserved. The city was rediscovered in 1911. No one really knows what Machu Picchu was used for. Not many people seem to have lived in its stone buildings. The city may have been used for religious rituals.

1533–1548

THE CONQUISTADORS

Diego de Almagro crossed the barren Atacama Desert during his two-year search for gold in what is now Chile.

The conquistadors were rough, brutal men. They included Pizarro's brothers, Hernando and Gonzalo, as well as Diego de Almagro. In 1533, Almagro nearly went to war with another conquistador, Pedro de Alvarado, for control of Ecuador. Alvarado finally backed down.

In 1535, the Spanish king sent Almagro south to set up the colony of New Toledo. Almagro explored for two years, but found no valuable land. When he tried to claim the city of Cuzco, he was defeated and executed by Hernando Pizarro. Almagro's supporters then assassinated Francisco Pizarro on June 26, 1541.

Power Crazy

Gonzalo Pizarro was in Amazonia, looking for valuable cinnamon trees. He rushed home and declared himself king of an independent Peru. In 1548, a Spanish army arrived to defeat him. His execution marked the end of the Pizarro family's 20-year rule.

CITY OF GOLD

El Dorado—"the gilded one"—was the name of a city said to be full of gold and other riches. A dream of finding the city drove many of the conquistadors on. But they were all disappointed. No evidence of the city has ever been found. For some conquistadors, the prize was another fabled place. This was named La Canela, a land said to be full of thick groves of cinnamon trees that produced a valuable spice. Again, it turned out not to exist. But some conquistadors grew rich from other resources, such as gold, silver, or even wood.

Pedro de Alvarado leads his men in Guatemala. He conquered large parts of Central America, including Guatemala, El Salvador, and Honduras.

DID YOU KNOW?

Gonzalo Pizarro took 4,000 natives into Amazonia in 1541. They all died of cold in the Andes or heat in the forest.

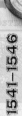

FRANCISCO DE ORELLANO

In 1541, Francisco de Orellana joined Gonzalo Pizarro in Amazonia, searching for La Canela. For months, they hacked through jungle looking for cinnamon trees. Their men gradually died from cold or from heat exhaustion. When the survivors ran short of food, Orellana set off to find supplies.

On the tributaries of the Amazon, native peoples still live in isolated villages on creeks and move around on boats made of wood or reeds.

DID YOU KNOW?

Orellana heard stories of the Amazons, a tribe of ferocious female warriors who gave their name to the river.

Orellana was the first European to travel through the dense rain forests of Amazonia on his way to the Atlantic. He was helped by friendly local peoples.

Orellana sailed on a barge down a small river. When he did not return, Pizarro assumed he was dead and went back to Peru. In fact, Orellana had found a much larger river: the Amazon. At a friendly village, he built himself a bigger ship. Then he sailed down the huge river for 3,000 miles (4,800 km), reaching the Atlantic Ocean in August 1542.

Governor of New Andalusia

Orellana made his way along the coast to Venezuela and then back to Spain. King Charles I made him governor of the region, which was named New Andalusia. He ordered Orellana to colonize the area. But Orellana died from disease as he explored the mouth of the Amazon in 1546.

IN COLOMBIA

Gonzalo Jiménez de Quesada searched for El Dorado in what is now northern Colombia. Unlike many Spaniards, he treated local people well and avoided bloodshed; he only lost four men during his conquest of the region. He founded Bogotá, now the capital of Colombia. He was still searching for El Dorado in his 60s, but never found the fabled city.

1535–1537

PEDRO DE MENDOZA

The plains of Argentina—the pampas—provided little food to support Mendoza on an expedition into the Inca Empire in Peru.

Unlike other conquistadors, Pedro de Mendoza was a nobleman at the Spanish court. In 1535, he led 12 ships and 1,500 men to the area around the Plate River (in present-day Argentina). At the river's mouth, Mendoza founded what would become the city of Buenos Aires.

DID YOU KNOW?

Buenos Aires means "good airs" or "fair winds." It got the name because its air smelled sweet to the explorers.

Mendoza hoped to head to Peru to look for gold. But the flat plains around Buenos Aires provided little food to support the explorers. There were few natives they could enslave to work on farms.

Driven Out

In frustration, Mendoza attacked some local people. The tribes defended themselves, killing many of the Spaniards and setting some of their ships on fire. With Buenos Aires in flames, the Spaniards faced starvation. Mendoza set sail for Spain in 1537, but died on the voyage from disease.

JUAN DE AYOLAS

When Mendoza left Buenos Aires for Spain in 1537, he left Juan de Ayolas in charge. Ayolas sailed up the Parana River and founded the settlement of Corpus Christi. He explored the Paraguay River and built a fort at Asunción. Ayolas then headed north into the forest—and was never heard from again.

The Capitol building in Buenos Aires: Mendoza founded the city but was forced to flee by the threat of starvation after clashes with local people.

1541–1553

PEDRO DEL VALDIVIA

Pedro de Valdivia was a veteran conquistador by the time he conquered Chile. He had fought in Venezuela and supported the Pizarros in Peru. The Spanish crown gave him permission to explore to the south of the Inca Empire.

A glacier flows into a fjord in the Strait of Magellan. Valdivia organized an expedition to sail the strait from the Pacific to the Atlantic Ocean.

Valdivia's achievement in bringing Chile into the Spanish Empire places him alongside the other major figures in the conquest of Latin America.

DID YOU KNOW?

In 1552, Valdivia organized the first European expedition to sail from west to east through the Strait of Magellan.

Unlike most conquistadors, Valdivia wanted to develop local resources. He also founded settlements along Chile's west coast.

Pushing South

From 1541, Valdivia followed Almagro's route through the Atacama Desert. Over years, he headed south to Santiago, now Chile's capital. He got as far south as the Bio Bio River and claimed the territory for Spain. In 1553, he was captured and killed by local Araucanian Indians.

VALDIVIA'S DEATH

For his exploration in Chile, Valdivia hired a local man, Lautaro, to work with his horses. The Spaniards' horses terrified many native peoples, but Lautaro learned all about them. He used his knowledge to plan a way to defeat the Spanish cavalry. The plan involved fighting on difficult terrain and tiring the horses out. It worked. The Spanish horsemen were defeated. Valdivia himself was captured and killed.

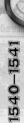
1540–1541

ÁLVAR NUÑEZ CABEZA DE VACA

Álvar Núñez Cabeza de Vaca was an experienced explorer. In 1527, he had been one of just four survivors out of 600 men who explored Florida. In 1540, the Spanish crown sent him to the Rio de la Plata colony (in present-day Argentina), which had a corrupt governor. Cabeza de Vaca arrived on Brazil's coast in 1541. He set out to the capital, Asunción.

Cabeza de Vaca's route to Asunción took him past the spectacular Iguaçu Falls on the Iguaçu River. He was the first European to see the falls.

This old map shows islands in the Caribbean and part of the coastline of South America, with the Tropic of Cancer.

Cabeza de Vaca marched 600 miles (965 km) to Asunción with 250 men and 26 horses. The journey along the Iguaçu and the Parana Rivers to the Paraguay River took four months. The men had to hack through thick rain forest.

Unpopular Reformer

In Asunción, Cabeza de Vaca stamped out the corruption. That made him unpopular. He left to explore more of the Paraguay River. When he returned, he was imprisoned by supporters of the corrupt leaders. They got the Spanish authorities to banish Cabeza de Vaca to Africa. He later described his travels in a book that influenced many later explorers.

DID YOU KNOW?

Cabeza de Vaca and his men were the first Europeans to see the Iguaçu Falls on the Brazil–Argentina border.

CATTLE FARMING

Many Europeans who went to Argentina in the 1580s went to farm ranches. The pampas—grasslands—were ideal for raising cattle. Unlike other colonists, they did not use slaves; they did the work themselves. They and their families settled permanently, making them true colonists.

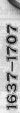

THE AMAZON

The Portuguese saw Brazil as less important than their colony in the East Indies. They did set up sugar plantations along the coast, which were worked by African slaves, but the Portuguese did not go far inland. It was left to missionaries and slave hunters to explore the vast Amazon River.

An Amazonian hunter prepares to kill a fish with a bow and arrow. Some Amazonian peoples still live as they did in the 17th century.

The tributaries of the Amazon provided Jesuit missionaries with relatively easy routes through the thick rain forest of the Amazonian basin.

DID YOU KNOW?

Brazil's modern boundaries largely agree with Teixeira's—breaking the Treaty of Tordesillas by 1,500 miles (2,400 km).

Slave hunters traveled as far as the Andes and the Paraguay River. They took Portuguese culture and language deep into the continent.

Mapping the Land

The Portuguese became anxious to map Brazil to stop the Spanish claiming any territory. In 1637, Pedro de Teixeira, an experienced cartographer, was sent to map the Amazon from its mouth to the Andes. He paddled up the river and along its tributaries. He then crossed the Andes to Quito (now in Ecuador), but the Spanish were suspicious and ordered him out of their territory.

THE AMAZON

The world's second-longest river—the largest in terms of water volume—begins as a tiny glacial stream high up in the ice-covered Andes Mountains. The river flows from Iquitos in Peru across Brazil to the Atlantic Ocean. It is so big that its basin covers 30 percent of South America and holds one-fifth of the world's total river flow. The river is over 6 miles (10 km) wide in places.

The scattered settlements of the Amazon proved welcoming for some missionaries but dangerous—even fatal—for others.

Teixeira went back to Brazil in 1639. He claimed more territory for Portugal, including the mouth of the Rio de Ora. Like earlier explorers, he heard reports about a tribe of female warriors, but he did not see them.

Minerals and Missionaries

In 1666, Agostinho Viale was put in charge of Brazil's mines. He set out into the Mato Grosso Plateau to seek emeralds. Viale reached Sierra das Esmeraldas, but died of malaria. However, the route he found allowed many more prospectors to exploit Brazil's mineral wealth.

Jesuits on the Amazon

The Jesuits explored much of Brazil as they set up missions throughout the country. The Czech, Samuel Fritz, for example, spent 20 years exploring the many tributaries of the Upper Amazon. He founded as many as 50 missions. In 1707, he produced a detailed map of the whole Amazon. Other Jesuits recorded the customs of the Amazonian peoples or the plants and animals they saw.

THE JESUITS

The Jesuit Order was a Catholic organization founded in 1534. It was organized along military lines to convert other peoples to Christianity. Jesuits first arrived in Latin America in 1549 and set up missions in Brazil, Paraguay, and Argentina. They went to remote places that others ignored. Their severe training prepared them to face difficult conditions and dangers.

This painting of a Jesuit priest is in a church in Concepción, in Chiquitos, Bolivia. The Jesuits founded many towns in Bolivia.

DID YOU KNOW?

In 1750, the Spanish agreed to Portugal's claim to most of central South America, which the Jesuits had mapped.

PRIVATEERS

The New World attracted many privateers. These sailors had licenses that enabled them to board foreign ships or to engage in smuggling. In many ways, they were pirates. Privateers helped other European countries to disrupt the Spanish and Portuguese empires.

British privateer John Hawkins tried to copy Portuguese smugglers in the 1560s, taking captive Africans to Brazil as slaves.

DID YOU KNOW?

Francis Drake was the first Englishman to gaze on the Pacific Ocean when he climbed a mountain in Panama.

This hill in Potosí, Bolivia, was home to a rich silver mine. The silver helped fund the Spanish Empire—but was also a target for the privateers.

THE PRIVATEERS

"Privateer" was a polite name for a pirate. In the 16th century, European rulers granted shipowners "letters of marque." The letters allowed them to attack any ship that flew the flag of an enemy country. French privateers operated along the Florida coast. They attacked Spanish ships in the Caribbean, which were often carrying gold or silver to Spain. British privateers also raided Spanish ports.

English privateers challenged the Spanish colonies in the Americas. King Philip II of Spain was furious. In 1562, John Hawkins offered to protect Spanish colonies from French privateers if he was allowed to trade freely himself. Philip refused his offer.

The English Attacked

Backed by Queen Elizabeth I of England, Hawkins set off on another voyage in October 1564. It became more difficult to make a profit. The Spanish king had threatened severe penalties for anyone trading with the English.

1562–1590

DID YOU KNOW?

Sir Walter Raleigh built the *Ark Royal*, the flagship of the English fleet that fought the Spanish Armada in 1588.

In 1595, Walter Raleigh explored rivers like the Orinoco in Venezuela in his search for the fabled land of El Dorado.

In 1567, Hawkins's ships were attacked by the Spanish in the Mexican port of San Juan de Ulua. Only one ship escaped.

Drake Fights Back

Hawkins's cousin, Francis Drake, was on the fleet. He vowed revenge. In 1572, Drake returned to Panama with two ships and 73 men. He attacked the Spanish territory and captured a convoy of gold. Drake spent six months raiding the Caribbean and returned to England in April 1573 with his vast booty.

An Englishman's Dream

Unlike Hawkins and Drake, Sir Walter Raleigh was less interested in gold than in founding a colony. He chose a site in North America, which he named "Virginia" for the "Virgin Queen," Elizabeth I. Raleigh founded a colony at Roanoke in 1585. It was attacked by Native Americans. When reinforcements arrived in 1590, the settlement was empty. The fate of the colonists remains a mystery.

SILVER

The discovery of silver in Mexico, Peru, and especially at Potosí in Bolivia made the Spanish very rich. The Spanish crown used the silver to pay for its colonies and armies, and pay off its debts. But the boom was short lived. The mines ran out, but the Spaniards had no industry at home. By the end of the 17th century, Spain had gone from being one of Europe's richest nations to one of its poorest.

Spanish treasure galleons were easy targets. Pirates and privateers were based on a part of the Caribbean coast known as the "Spanish Main."

1798–1803

ALEXANDER VON HUMBOLDT

German-born scientist Alexander von Humboldt traveled throughout Central and South America. His discoveries were unrivaled. In just four years, he and the French botanist, Aimé Bonpland, traveled 6,000 miles (9,650 km). They discovered thousands of previously unknown species of plants and animals.

Among the botanical riches of the Amazon was rubber. It is "tapped" from trees by cutting the bark and collecting the latex that runs out.

DID YOU KNOW?

The eminent British scientist Charles Darwin called Humboldt "the greatest scientific traveler who ever lived."

Alexander von Humboldt was the first of a generation of scientific explorers to study the riches of South America's natural world.

ISABEL GODIN

In 1769, Isabel Godin des Odonais set off from Ecuador to meet her husband. He was a scientist in Guiana. The Spanish authorities would not let him return to Ecuador. The journey was a disaster. Of the 42 people who set out, Isabel was the only survivor. She was alone in the jungle for nine days before local people rescued her. She finally reached Guiana and was reunited with her husband. She had traveled 3,000 miles (4,830 km) down the Amazon; she was the first woman ever to do so.

The travels began in 1798. The Spanish king, Charles IV, gave Humboldt and Bonpland permission to carry out scientific surveys of his territory in Latin America. The next year, the scientists arrived in Venezuela.

An Amazing Journey

Their first goal was to explore the Orinoco River in Venezuela. Sailing to the upper reaches of the river, the two men corrected mistakes in the maps they had brought with them. Humboldt then canoed along the Casiquiare River to the Rio Negro. He showed that the Orinoco and Amazon river systems were connected.

Humboldt and Bonpland spent the winter in Cuba. They collected many plant species, including more than 6,000 previously unknown ones.

In South America

In 1801, the two scientists traveled to Quito (in present-day Ecuador) via the Magdalena River from Colombia. Their next adventure was to climb Mount Chimborazo in the Andes. They reached 19,000 feet (5,800 m) before turning back because of a lack of oxygen. That set a world record for the highest climb ever made up to that time.

Although they did not reach the top of Mount Chimborazo, the explorers climbed higher than anyone else had previously.

DID YOU KNOW?

The cold north-flowing ocean current off Chile was named the Humboldt Current in honor of the explorer.

This painting by Eduard Ender shows Humboldt and Bonpland cataloging some of their many discoveries in a hut in the rain forest.

Final Trips

Humboldt and Bonpland then traveled to Lima, Peru. On the way, they crossed the Atacama Desert of Chile. Humboldt explained how a cold ocean current kept the desert cool but dry. The men then sailed to Mexico in 1803 to make some more studies. Back in Europe, Humboldt described his discoveries in a 23-volume study. The work became a vital reference for any explorer traveling to South America.

QUININE

One of the main obstacles to European explorers in hot climates was malaria. The disease, which is transmitted by mosquito bites, killed many Europeans in Africa, Asia, and South America. In the mid-19th century, explorers realized that native peoples in the Andes used the bark of the cinchona tree to protect themselves from malaria. The bark produced a drug named quinine. If taken properly, it provided immunity from malaria.

1820–1925

SCIENTIFIC EXPLORERS

After Humboldt and Bonpland's pioneering journeys, many scientists arrived in South America. They still faced dangers, but the rich natural life of the region drew European naturalists. They found species of plants and animals there that did not exist anywhere else.

In 1848, Englishmen Henry Walter Bates and Alfred Russell Wallace collected remarkable butterflies and insects in the Amazon basin.

DID YOU KNOW?

Francisco Moreno, a professor from Argentina, was one of the few 19th-century scientific explorers from America.

The plants of the rain forest are still providing valuable new drugs after more than a century of scientific investigation of the Amazon region.

Plants from the Amazon rain forest amazed 19th-century European botanists. In 1820, the German Carl Friedrich Phillipp von Martius and zoologist Johann Baptist von Spix collected 6,500 plant and 3,300 animal specimens to take to Europe.

Exploring the Amazon

In 1849, Kew Gardens in London sent the botanist Richard Spruce to the Amazon. He collected seeds from the cinchona tree so that quinine could be produced in Britain's colony in India. When he returned home in 1864, he took 30,000 botanical specimens. He had also recorded 21 separate local languages and mapped many rivers.

A LOST EXPLORER

The English soldier Percy Fawcett spent 20 years exploring Bolivia, Brazil, Peru, and Paraguay. In 1925, he read about the "lost cities" of the Amazon. Fawcett set out to find them with his son—but the two men disappeared into the Brazilian rain forest. Two search parties went to look for them, but no trace of them was ever found.

GLOSSARY

botanist A scientist who studies plants and their uses.

cartographer A person who studies and draws maps.

cinnamon A valuable spice obtained from the bark of the cinnamon tree.

colony A settlement founded in one territory by people from another country.

conquistadors Spanish for "conquerors"; adventurers who went to the Americas hoping to gain riches and glory.

continent A large landmass.

decree An announcement or ruling that has the same effect as a law.

expedition A journey made for a particular purpose.

governor Someone who runs a colony on behalf of a ruler or government.

interpreter Someone who translates what someone else is saying into another language.

isthmus A narrow strip of land that connects two larger landmasses.

missionary A person who preaches in order to persuade other people to convert to a religion.

naturalist A scientist who studies or collects plants and animals.

privateer A ship's captain with written authority to seize the ships of other countries.

strait A narrow stretch of water connecting two larger bodies of water.

treaty A formal agreement between two or more countries.

tributary A smaller river that runs into a bigger one.

veteran Someone who has long experience of doing something.

FURTHER INFORMATION

Books

Abrams, Dennis. *El Dorado* (Lost Worlds and Mysterious Civilizations). Chelsea House Publishers, 2012.

DiConsiglio, John. *Francisco Pizzaro: Destroyer of the Inca Empire* (Wicked History). Scholastic, Inc., 2008.

Green, Carl L. *Cortés: Conquering the Powerful Aztec Empire* (Great Explorers of the World). Enslow Publishers, 2010.

Hoogenboom, Lynn. *Francisco Pizzaro: A Primary Source Biography* (The Primary Source Library of Famous Explorers). PowerKids Press, 2006.

Nick, Charles. *Sir Francis Drake: Slave Trader and Pirate* (Wicked History). Scholastic, Inc., 2009.

Ollhoff, Jim. *The Conquistadors* (Hispanic American History). Abdo Publishing, 2011.

Websites

http://www.enchantedlearning. com/explorers/samerica.shtml
Enchanted Learning directory of explorers.

http://www.pbs.org/opb/ conquistadors/home.htm
Site accompanying PBS series, with full curriculum resources.

http://www.bbc.co.uk/history/ british/tudors/conquistadors_01. shtml
BBC History site about the Spanish conquistadors.

Publisher's note to educators and parents: Our editors have carefully reviewed these websites to ensure that they are suitable for students. Many websites change frequently, however, and we cannot guarantee that a site's future contents will continue to meet our high standards of quality and educational value. Be advised that students should be closely supervised whenever they access the Internet.

INDEX